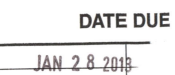

Barack Obama
44th U.S. President

Written by **Joeming Dunn**   Illustrated by **Rod Espinosa**

magic
Wagon

visit us at www.abdopublishing.com

Published by Magic Wagon, a division of the ABDO Publishing Group, 8000 West 78th Street, Edina, Minnesota 55439. Copyright © 2012 by Abdo Consulting Group, Inc. International copyrights reserved in all countries. All rights reserved. No part of this book may be reproduced in any form without written permission from the publisher.

Graphic Planet™ is a trademark and logo of Magic Wagon.

Printed in the United States of America, North Mankato, Minnesota.
042011
092011
This book contains at least 10% recycled materials.

Written by Joeming Dunn
Illustrated and colored by Rod Espinosa
Lettered by Rod Espinosa
Edited by Stephanie Hedlund and Rochelle Baltzer
Interior layout and design by Antarctic Press
Cover art by Rod Espinosa
Cover design by Abbey Fitzgerald

Library of Congress Cataloging-in-Publication Data

Dunn, Joeming W.
  Barack Obama : 44th U.S. president / written by Joeming Dunn ; illustrated by Rod Espinosa.
       p. cm. -- (Presidents of the United States bio-graphics)
  Includes index.
  ISBN 978-1-61641-648-5
  1. Obama, Barack--Juvenile literature. 2. Presidents--United States--Biography--Juvenile literature. 3. Racially mixed people--United States--Biography--Juvenile literature. 4. Obama, Barack--Comic books, strips, etc. 5. Presidents--United States--Biography--Comic books, strips, etc. 6. Racially mixed people--United States--Biography--Comic books, strips, etc. 7. Graphic novels. I. Espinosa, Rod, ill. II. Title.
  E908.D86 2012
  973.932092--dc22
  [B]
                              2011010669

Table of Contents

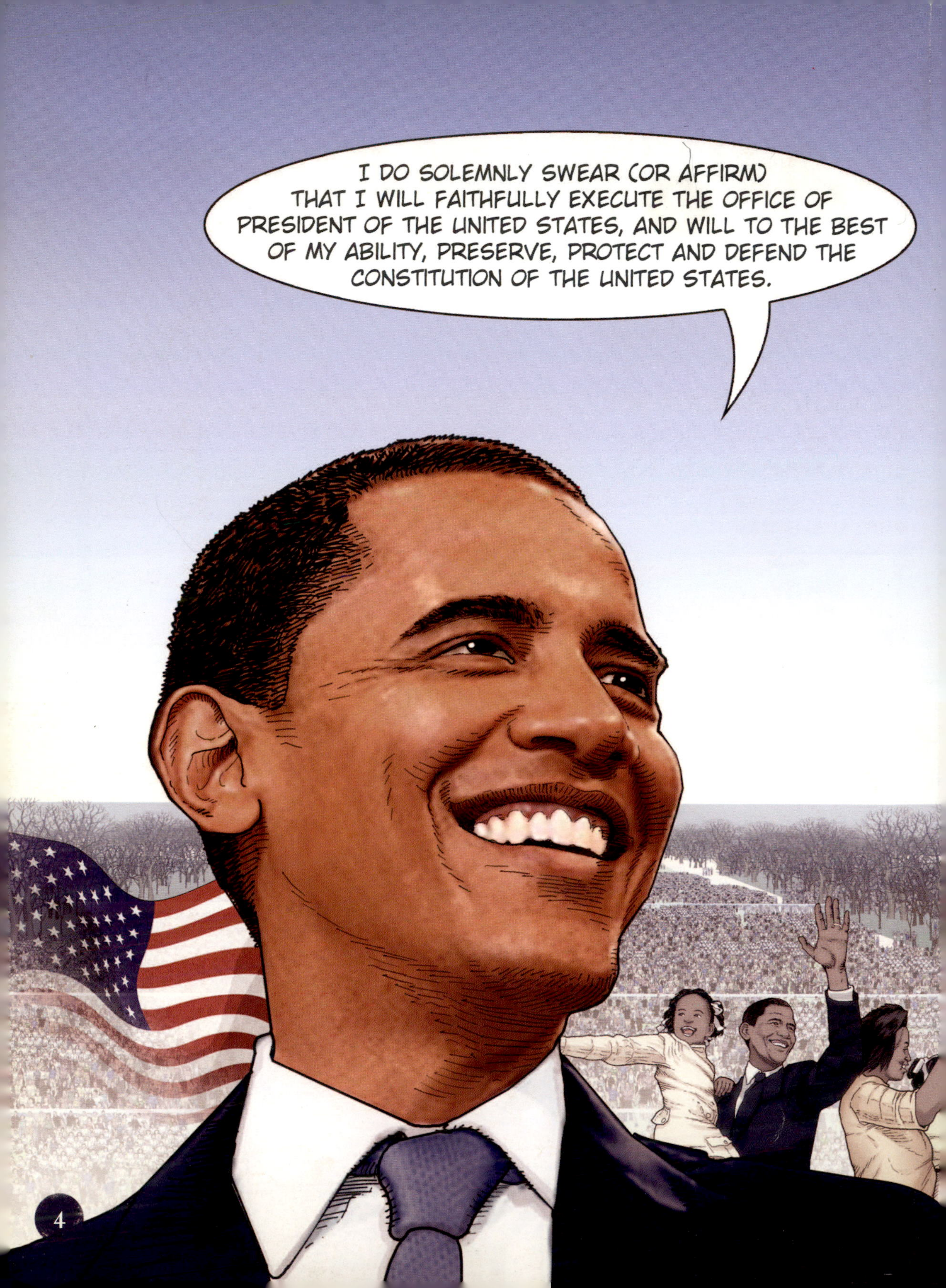
I DO SOLEMNLY SWEAR (OR AFFIRM) THAT I WILL FAITHFULLY EXECUTE THE OFFICE OF PRESIDENT OF THE UNITED STATES, AND WILL TO THE BEST OF MY ABILITY, PRESERVE, PROTECT AND DEFEND THE CONSTITUTION OF THE UNITED STATES.

Barack Hussein Obama was born on August 4, 1961, in Honolulu, Hawaii. His parents were Ann Dunham and Barack Obama Sr.

When Barack was two years old, his father left to go to school to get his PhD. Soon after, his parents divorced.

After the divorce, Barack Sr. moved to Kenya and remarried. Sadly, he died in an auto accident in 1982.

Barack's mother remarried in 1966 to Lolo Soetoro. They soon moved to Jakarta, Indonesia. Not long after the family moved, Barack's half sister Maya was born.

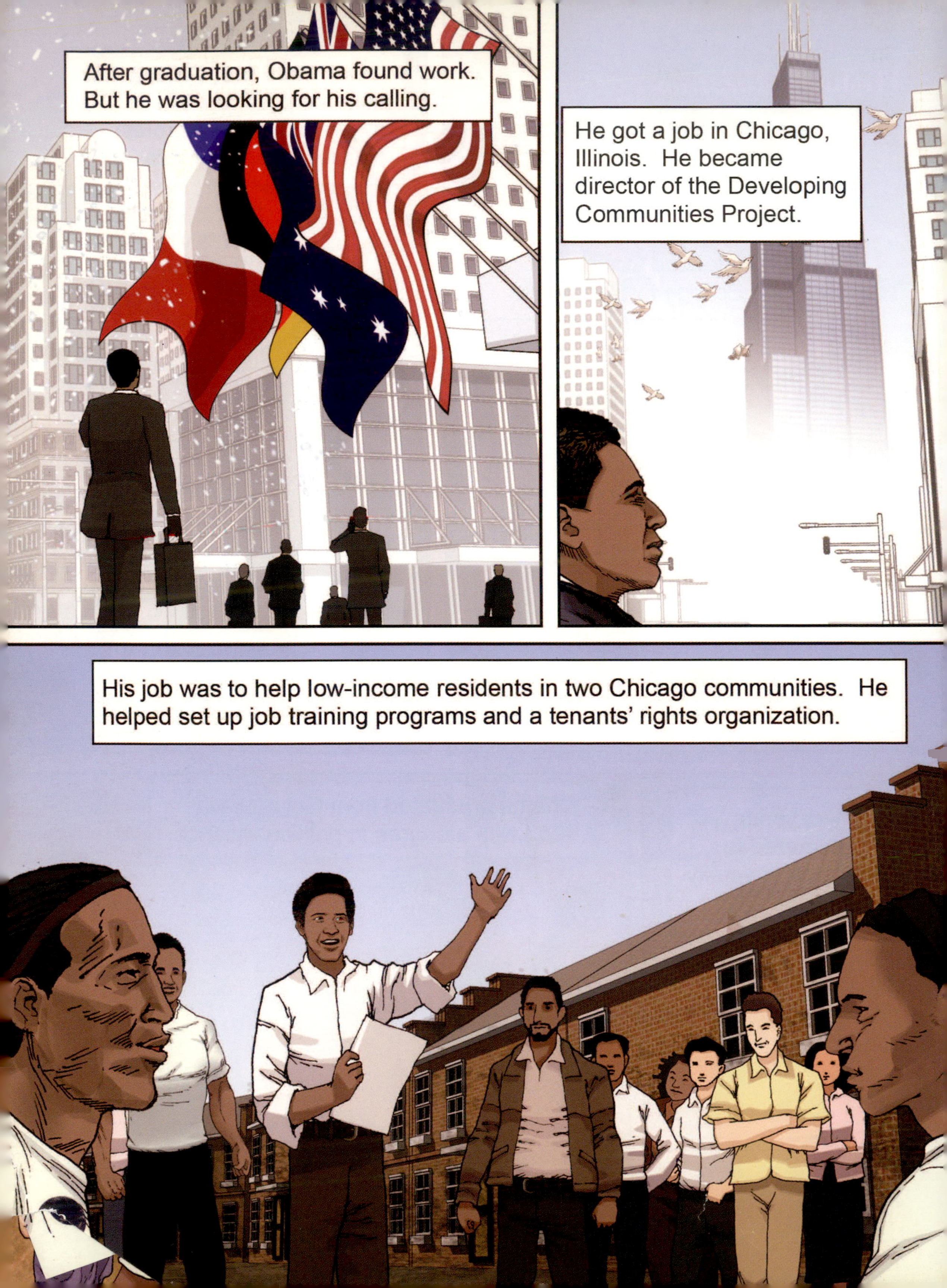
After graduation, Obama found work. But he was looking for his calling.
He got a job in Chicago, Illinois. He became director of the Developing Communities Project.
His job was to help low-income residents in two Chicago communities. He helped set up job training programs and a tenants' rights organization.

In 1988, Obama entered Harvard Law School.

During his time at Harvard, Obama became the first African-American president of the *Harvard Law Review*. He graduated with highest honors in 1991.

The next summer, Obama worked as an intern at a law firm in Chicago. He met an associate at the firm, Michelle Robinson.

They began dating. On October 3, 1992, they were married. They had two daughters, Malia and Sasha.

The Obamas settled in Chicago. Obama accepted a position teaching at the University of Chicago Law School.

Obama remained active in the community. In 1992, he helped organize a voter registration drive for the presidential election.

He also joined a law firm that specialized in civil rights cases.

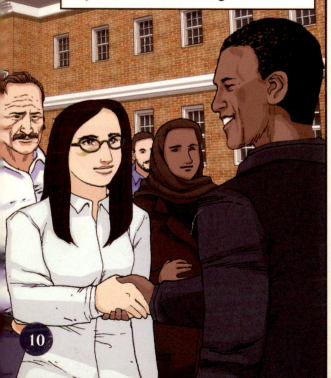

In 1995, his autobiography was published. It was called *Dreams from My Father: A Story of Race and Inheritance*.

In 1996, Obama ran for the Illinois State Senate. His work in the community helped him win the seat.

During his time as a state senator, he tried to work with both Democrats and Republicans.

He helped expand health care services.

He also increased tax credits for the working poor and got funding for child care.

In 2000, Obama ran for the U.S. House of Representatives. He was running against Bobby Rush. Unfortunately, Obama lost.

His loss in the election did not stop him.

Obama began to consider a run for the U.S. Senate in 2004. He hired political consultant David Axelrod. They began a strategy for a Senate run.

It was a wide-open contest with many candidates. Obama easily won the Democratic nomination.

12

Obama was becoming a rising star in the Democratic Party. He was chosen to give a keynote speech in the 2004 Democratic National Convention.

WITH JUST A CHANGE IN PRIORITIES, WE CAN MAKE SURE THAT EVERY CHILD IN AMERICA HAS A DECENT SHOT AT LIFE, AND THAT THE DOORS OF OPPORTUNITY REMAIN OPEN TO ALL.

Obama expected a difficult campaign against Republican Jack Ryan. But a scandal forced Ryan to withdraw from the race.

Obama easily won the election. He became the third African-American to be elected to the U.S. Senate since the Reconstruction.

Ryan was replaced with former presidential candidate Alan Keyes.

Obama was sworn in as a senator on January 4, 2005.

He cosponsored a bill to reduce weapons of mass destruction in Europe.

He helped establish a Web site to help track federal spending.

$$$$$

Obama held many assignments in the Senate. He sat on the committees for Foreign Relations and Veterans' Affairs.

While in the Senate, Obama wrote his second book. It told readers his vision of America's future.

After the book's release, it was number one on the *New York Times* and Amazon.com best-sellers lists.

In February 2007, Obama sensed an opportunity. It was nearing the end of George W. Bush's presidency. The election was wide open for Democratic and Republican candidates.

On February 10, Obama announced his candidacy for the 2008 presidential election.

I KNOW I HAVEN'T SPENT A LOT OF TIME LEARNING THE WAYS OF WASHINGTON, BUT I'VE BEEN THERE LONG ENOUGH TO KNOW THAT THE WAYS OF WASHINGTON MUST CHANGE.

Many Democratic candidates entered the race. But, soon only Obama, Hillary Rodham Clinton, and John Edwards remained.

Soon Edwards dropped out. Hillary Clinton was thought to be the favorite of the Democratic Party. She had been a member of the party for a long time. She was also the wife of former President Bill Clinton.

Obama needed a way to reach people. He decided to try to start a grassroots movement.

He used the Internet to get his message out and to raise money for his campaign.

Both candidates won key states. At the end of the primaries, neither had enough delegates to get the nomination.

But, Obama had more delegates. So, Clinton ended her campaign. She stood behind Obama for the Democratic candidate for president.

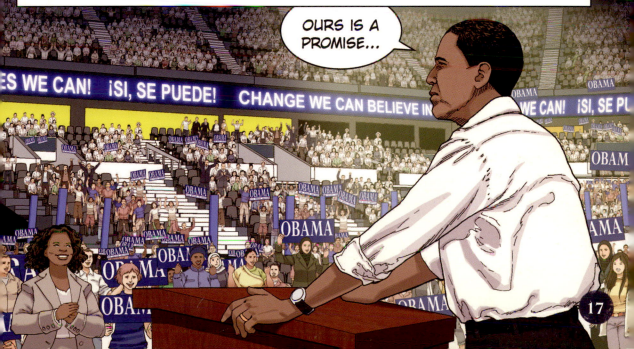

Obama accepted the nomination. He delivered his acceptance speech at INVESCO Field in Denver, Colorado. He spoke before a crowd of over 75,000.

OURS IS A PROMISE...

Obama's Republican opponent was Senator John McCain of Arizona. McCain picked the popular governor of Alaska, Sarah Palin, as his running mate.

COUNTRY FIRST

Obama chose Senator Joe Biden of Delaware as his running mate.

Obama had set up a large network during the primaries. He was up to the challenge of the upcoming election.

Obama's campaign set fund-raising records. He was the first major party presidential candidate to decline public financing since its creation in 1976.

Businessmen for Obama
Bricklayers for Obama
Nurses for Obama
Athletes for Obama
Engineers for Obama
Musicians for Obama
Actors for Obama
Lawyers for Obama
Artists for Obama
Carpenters for Obama

Doctors for Obama
Scientists for Obama
Knitters for Obama
Architects for Obama
Directors for Obama
Drivers for Obama

Astronomists for Obama
Botanists for Obama
Photographers for Obama
Writers for Obama
Salesmen for Obama
Realtors for Obama

OBAMA 08

Obama was able to connect with many voters and get across his message of change.

In addition, Palin had become the target of many people. Some questioned her ability to be vice president.

On November 4, 2008, Election Day had arrived.

As polls closed, the election seemed uncertain.

But as the evening went on, things changed. "Swing" states that had voted Republican in the last election went to Obama.

At the end of the night, Obama received 365 electoral votes to McCain's 173. Obama had won the election.

| Democrat | 365 |
| Republican | 173 |

TOTAL ELECTORAL VOTES

On January 20, 2009, Barack Obama was sworn in as the 44th President of the United States. He became the first African-American to be elected president.

Some estimate more than a million people gathered to watch Obama take the oath of office.

IN REAFFIRMING THE GREATNESS OF OUR NATION, WE UNDERSTAND THAT GREATNESS IS NEVER A GIVEN. IT MUST BE EARNED.

Obama quickly chose his Administration. It contained experienced people and some new to Washington. He named Hillary Clinton his Secretary of State. He also appointed Sonia Sotomayor, who was the first Hispanic justice on the Supreme Court.

When Obama took office, he needed to deal with many problems right away.

The nation and world were in the middle of an economic recession. Many people had lost their jobs and houses.

JOB FAIR

FOR SALE

One of his first acts provided money to stabilize the financial markets.

It also gave loans to large companies while they reorganized.

BANK

Obama also inherited two wars, one in Iraq and the other in Afghanistan. Both were fighting against terrorism.

Because of the wars, the United States was isolated from the rest of the world. Obama sent Vice President Joe Biden and Secretary of State Hillary Clinton to many countries. Their job was to help begin a new era in foreign relations.

Obama even tried to open the door for relations with Islamic nations. To do this, he gave a speech on Arabic Television promoting peace.

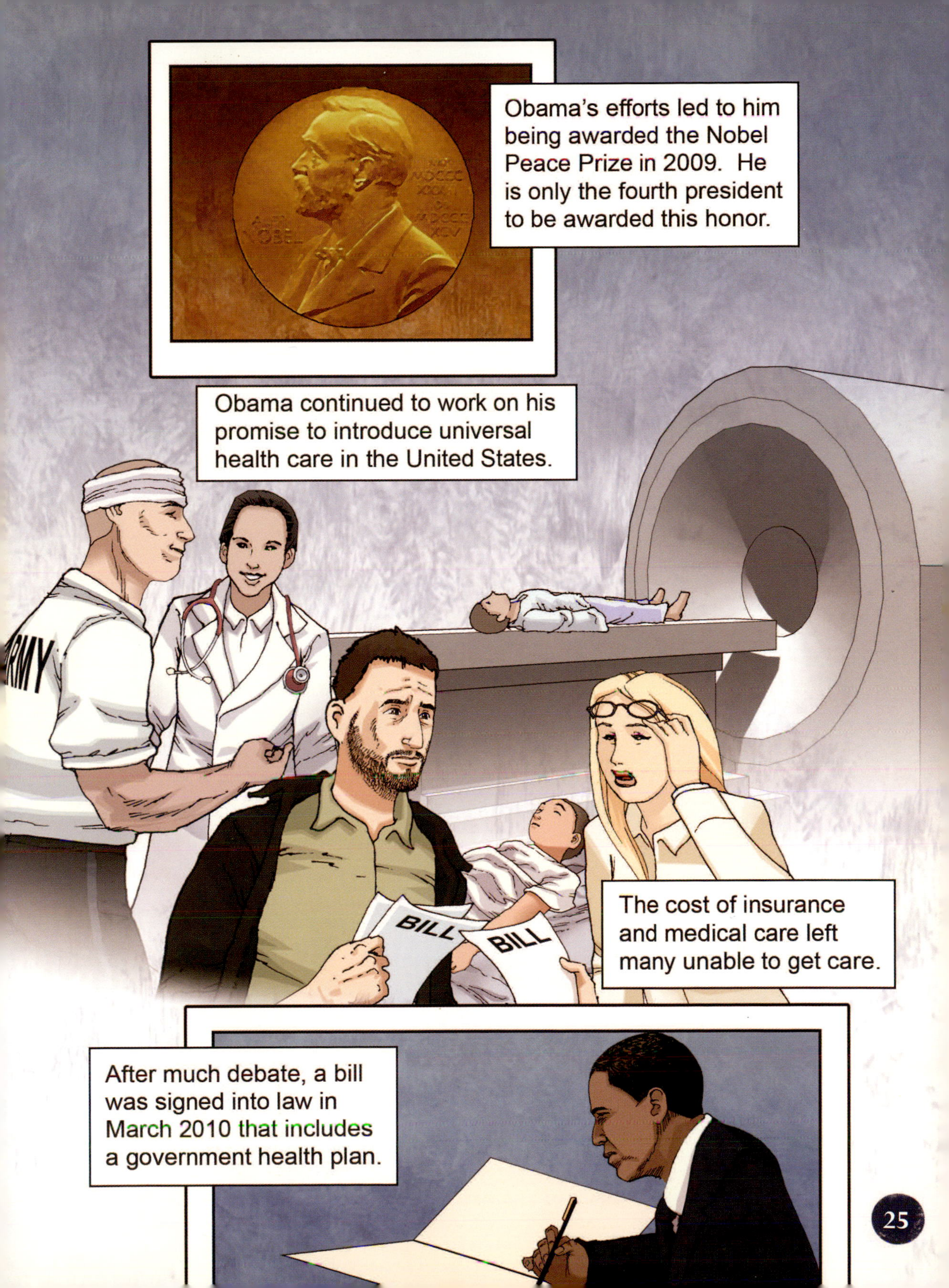
Obama's efforts led to him being awarded the Nobel Peace Prize in 2009. He is only the fourth president to be awarded this honor.
Obama continued to work on his promise to introduce universal health care in the United States.
BILL
BILL
The cost of insurance and medical care left many unable to get care.
After much debate, a bill was signed into law in March 2010 that includes a government health plan.

Obama continues to face challenges. In April 2010, an offshore oil well exploded in the Gulf of Mexico near Louisiana.

For 90 days, the well released millions of gallons of oil into the gulf. This caused an economic and environmental disaster.

Many believe Obama has not done enough for the economy. The United States is still experiencing high levels of unemployment...

...and the national debt is increasing.

9,000,000,999,999,100,000

HOMELESS VETERAN PLEASE HELP

On September 11, 2001, a terrorist group called al-Qaeda arranged an attack on the United States. They were able to crash four planes, damage the Pentagon, and destroy both towers of the World Trade Center.

The leader of al-Qaeda was a man named Osama bin Laden. He was the most wanted man in the world.

Using years of research, the United States identified one of bin Laden's most trusted messengers. They soon discovered bin Laden's location in Pakistan. President Obama ordered a raid of bin Laden's compound on May 1, 2011. During the 40-minute raid, bin Laden was killed.

Weeks before the raid, President Barack Obama had officially announced his plans to run for reelection in the 2012 Presidential election.

LET'S SEIZE THIS MOMENT TO START ANEW, TO CARRY THE DREAM FORWARD AND STRENGTHEN OUR UNION ONCE MORE.

Obama continues to face tough challenges during his presidency. He would like politicians to focus on making positive changes. He has also asked the American people not to quit even through these difficulties.

Fast Facts

Name - Barack Hussein Obama   Born - August 4, 1961

Wife - Michelle Robinson (1964–)   Children - 2

Political Party - Democrat

Age at Inauguration - 47   Years Served - 2009–present

Vice President - Joe Biden

President Obama's Cabinet

First term - January 20, 2009–Present

State – Hillary Rodham Clinton

Treasury – Timothy F. Geithner

Defense – Robert M. Gates

Attorney General – Eric H. Holder Jr.

Interior – Kenneth L. Salazar

Agriculture – Thomas J. Vilsack

Commerce – Gary F. Locke

Labor – Hilda L. Solis

Health and Human Services – Kathleen Sebelius

Housing and Urban Development – Shaun L.S. Donovan

Transportation – Ray LaHood

Energy – Steven Chu

Education – Arne Duncan

Veterans Affairs – Eric K. Shinseki

Homeland Security – Janet A. Napolitano

The Office of the President

- To be president, a person must meet three requirements. He or she must be at least 35 years old and a natural-born U.S. citizen. A candidate must also have lived in the United States for at least 14 years.

- The U.S. presidential election is an indirect election. Voters from each state elect representatives called electors for the Electoral College. The number of electors is based on population. Each elector pledges to cast their vote for the candidate who receives the highest number of popular votes in their state. A candidate must receive the majority of Electoral College votes to win.

- Each president may be elected to two four-year terms. The presidential election is held on the Tuesday after the first Monday in November. The president is sworn in on January 20 of the following year.

- While in office, the president receives a salary of $400,000 each year. He or she lives in the White House and has 24-hour Secret Service protection. When the president leaves office, he or she receives Secret Service protection for ten more years. He or she also receives a yearly pension of $191,300 and funding for office space, supplies, and staff.

Timeline

1961 - Barack Hussein Obama was born to Ann Dunham and Barack Obama Sr. on August 4.

1983 - Obama graduated from Columbia University.

1988 - Obama enrolled at Harvard Law School, where he was elected as the first African-American president of the *Harvard Law Review*.

1991 - Obama graduated from Harvard Law School.

1992 - Obama married Michelle Robinson.

1995 - Obama published his autobiography, *Dreams From My Father*.

1996 - Obama won the Illinois State Senate seat as a Democrat.

2004 - Obama became the third African-American elected to the Senate since the Reconstruction.

2005 - Obama was sworn in as a U.S. Senator on January 4.

2007 - Obama announced he would run for president on February 10.

2008 - Obama won the presidential election by 365 to 173 electoral votes on November 4.

2009 - On January 20, Obama was sworn in as the 44th President of the United States; on October 8, Obama was awarded the Nobel Peace Prize.

2010 - Obama signed a health care bill into law.

Web Sites

To learn more about Barack Obama, visit ABDO Publishing Group online at **www.abdopublishing.com**. Web sites about Obama are featured on our Book Links page. These links are routinely monitored and updated to provide the most current information available.

Glossary

academic - relating to school or education.

Administration - the people who manage a presidential government.

autobiography - a story of a person's life that is written by himself or herself.

campaign - to give speeches and state ideas in order to be voted into an elected office.

debt - something owed to someone, especially money.

delegate - a person chosen to represent others.

Democrat - a member of the Democratic political party. Democrats believe in social change and strong government.

Democratic National Convention - a national meeting held every four years. During the convention, the Democratic political party chooses its candidates for president and vice president.

grassroots movement - a political movement that grows through the actions of ordinary people.

heritage - something handed down from one generation to the next.

intern - a student or graduate gaining guided practical experience in a professional field.

keynote speech - a speech given to a group that gives the main issues important to those gathered.

Nobel Prize - any of six annual awards given to people who have made the greatest contributions to mankind. The prizes are awarded for physics, chemistry, medicine, economics, literature, and peace.

PhD - doctor of philosophy. Usually, this is the highest degree a student can earn.

primary - a method of selecting candidates to run for public office. A political party holds an election among its own members. They select the party members who will represent it in the coming general election.

recession - a period of time when business activity slows.

Republican - a member of the Republican political party. Republicans are conservative and believe in small government.

running mate - a person running for a lower-rank position on an election ticket. The candidate for vice president is the running mate of the candidate for president.

scandal - an action that shocks people and disgraces those connected with it.

strategy - a careful plan or method.

tenant - someone who rents or lease a home.

weapons of mass destruction - a weapon that can kill or harm a large amount of people at the same time.

Index